PANCAKES

A to Z

THE A TO Z COOKBOOK SERIES
BY MARIE SIMMONS

Bar Cookies A to Z

Muffins A to Z

Pancakes A to Z

PANCAKES

Marie Simmons

Photography by David Lazarus

Calligraphy by Richard High

A Chapters Book

HOUGHTON MIFFLIN COMPANY
BOSTON   NEW YORK
1997

For information about permission to reproduce selections from this book, write to Permissions,
Houghton Mifflin Company, 215 Park Avenue South, New York, New York 10003.

Library of Congress Cataloging-in-Publication Data

Simmons, Marie.
Pancakes A to Z / Marie Simmons; photography by David Lazarus; calligraphy by
Richard High.
       p.   cm — (The A to Z cookbook series)
Includes index.
ISBN 1-57630-043-9 (hardcover)
1. Pancakes, waffles, etc. I. Title. II. Series.
TX770.P34S555 1997
641.8'15—dc21   97-13767

Printed and bound in Italy
SFE 10 9 8 7 6 5 4 3 2 1

Designed by Susan McClellan

Front cover: Sweet Corn Cakes (page 76) by David Lazarus
Food stylist: Susan Ehlich
Prop stylist: Laura Hart

THIS BOOK IS DEDICATED to the memory of my father, Patrick Thomas Mataraza, Sr., and my brother, Patrick Thomas Mataraza, Jr., both loyal members of their hometown volunteer fire companies. When we were children, our father flipped pancakes at the annual firemen's pancake breakfast. A generation later, my brother continued the tradition for his own children.

Acknowledgments

THANK YOU, RUX MARTIN AND BARRY ESTABROOK, my editor and publisher, for your commitment to the A to Z series, and for making it mine. Thank you, Judith Weber, my agent, for invaluable guidance and encouragement. Thank you, Stacy Sussman, for flipping pancakes by my side, patiently testing and retesting, until we got them right. Thank you, Susan McClellan, for your enduring design. Thank you, Rose Grant, for your perfect index, both this time and retroactively for all the other times as well. Thank you, Jessica Sherman, for all your patient corrections. Last, but certainly not least, thank you, John, for your devotion, and for never saying (even when you were thinking it), "Pancakes, again?"

The Pancake Alphabet

A *is for*

B *is for*

C *is for*

D is for
Dutch Baby with Cardamom Honey Apples   34

E is for
Egg Pancake   36

F is for
Fresh Corn Cakes with Tomato Salsa   38
Flannel Cakes with Raspberry Maple Syrup   40

G is for
Ginger, Carrot & Sesame Pancakes   42

H is for
Heavenly Cloud Cakes   44

I is for
Indian Spiced Red Lentil Cakes with Coconut Raita   46

J is for
John's Crepes with Mushrooms, Spinach & Cheese   49
John's Basic Crepes   51

K is for
Kaiserschmarren with Plum Compote   53
(Emperor's Scrambled Pancake)

L is for

Luscious Lemon Pancakes   56

Latkes   58
(Potato Pancakes)

Little Crunchy Rice Pancakes   59

M is for

Mashed Potato Pancakes   60

N is for

New Year's Eve Popover Pancake with
Smoked Salmon & Dill Butter   62

O is for

Onion & Cumin Crepe   64

P is for

Pecan Pancakes with Buttered Pecans & Warm Maple Syrup   66

Q is for

Quinoa & Company Pancakes   68

R is for

Rux's Family's Favorite Pancakes   70

Rich Raspberry Sour Cream Pancakes   72

Introduction

FOR CHILDREN GROWING UP IN THE SLEEPY HAMLET of Milton, New York, the volunteer firemen's pancake breakfast ranked just behind Christmas as the most anticipated day of the year. Inside the red brick firehouse, long tables would be set up, draped in white paper and surrounded by rickety wooden chairs. Outside waited the fire engines, splendidly polished, all shiny red and sparkling chrome, winking in the spring sunlight.

For the other kids in the town, what was outside was clearly the main attraction. But for me, this was a food event of the highest order. I would sit patiently, watching and waiting, while my father and the other firemen, dressed in long white aprons and white paper chef's hats, milled about in the kitchen. Finally, the platters of round, floppy pancakes were brought to the table, and I could dig in. They were soaked in butter and luxuriating in maple syrup. I ate slowly, making them last.

For my brother and his friends, the Big Moment came when the fire chief sounded his shrill whistle. Shoving back from the table, they abandoned their half-eaten pancakes, tipping over chairs in the process. They thundered out the door, jockeying for position, jamming on heavy firemen's helmets, which comically covered their faces. They clambered up the fire trucks, clanging the bells, shrieking the sirens, on their way to extinguish a pretend five-alarm blaze.

Meanwhile, back inside, the station was blissfully quiet. Alone at the table, I enjoyed every last bite of my pancakes.

My brother followed in my father's footsteps and became fire chief. I pursued an equally exciting if somewhat less urgent calling: eating, cooking and studying foods from around the world. But those firehouse mornings must have lodged in my mind, because almost without knowing it, I amassed a fat file of pancake recipes in the process of my other research.

TODAY, I STILL LOVE PANCAKES AS MUCH AS I EVER DID, not just for their taste, but because they are quick and easy to make and because they are one of the most versatile foods I have ever encountered. They can be appetizers, main dishes or accompaniments. They can even be dessert. And although I will forever associate them with small-town America, they are a much-beloved food everywhere in the world, from the crisp lentil patties of southern India to the buckwheat blini of Russia and the delicate crepes of France.

The basic formula for the popular All-American pancake (also called a flapjack, hot cake or griddle cake) is a simple mixture of flour, milk, eggs, leavening, butter or vegetable oil and perhaps a little sugar. From this point on, the variations are endless. Use buttermilk instead of plain milk, and the pancake acquires a lovely lift. Add beer instead of milk, and the pancake becomes especially light, with a pleasant yeasty taste. Made with sour cream, cottage cheese, applesauce or yogurt, the pancake is by turns rich, tender, sweetly moist or tangy. Instead of using whole eggs, the whites can be beaten separately and folded into the batter, making pancakes that are light, fluffy and soft as clouds. And finally, the flour need not be wheat, but can be a mixture of grains: wheat germ, yellow or white cornmeal, oatmeal or buckwheat, to name just a few. You can add fresh fruit in season, dried fruits, spices, nuts or whatever happens to be on hand.

Some of my favorite recipes are patterned after the earliest pancakes made on this continent. Long before Dutch settlers brought pancakes to the New World, Native Americans patted ground corn into flat cakes and cooked them on hot stones. Variations range from sophisticated tiny pancakes served with a topping of sour cream and crowned with a smidgen of caviar that I serve as hors d'oeuvres to the homier Sweet Corn Pancakes, a popular breakfast at our house on lazy weekend mornings.

Whether you're feeding would-be firemen on the run or weekend idlers, all these pancakes are delicious enough to keep family, friends and guests around the table for second and third helpings.

Making Perfect Pancakes

ALTHOUGH PANCAKES ARE EASY TO MAKE—provided you use the proper measuring cup (see page 15)—cooking them requires a little know-how and patience. Common complaints are that the pancakes are burned, greasy or raw inside or sometimes, all of the above. Following these four rules should ensure perfect results:

1. Heat the pan first.

Pancakes should always be cooked on a hot,

preheated surface. Preheat the griddle or skillet over medium heat. Test the heat by adding a drop or two of water. The surface is hot enough when the water sizzles for a second and then evaporates. Now the skillet is ready to be coated with the fat of choice.

2. Choose the right fat—and use the right amount.

My preference is to brush the pan with a thin layer of vegetable oil once the pan is hot and before I cook the first batch. Whatever fat you choose, make sure it is minimal. Pancakes should be cooked on a fairly dry surface with just enough fat to moisten it and discourage sticking. There is usually enough in the batter to keep the surface moist (and greased) for subsequent batches; it is rarely necessary to add more after the first application. You can also spray the pan lightly with nonstick spray.

Never use ordinary butter, because the milk solids will burn. Butter burns at 250°F; pancakes cook at about 300° to 325°F. For a buttery taste, use clarified butter, which has a much higher smoking point. *To make clarified butter*, heat butter over low heat until the milk solids separate from the fat and sink to the bottom of the pan. Skim off the clarified butter and lightly brush it on the griddle or skillet.

3. Never rush pancakes.

A rushed pancake, though brown on the outside, will be underdone inside. Let the pancakes cook slowly until tiny bubbles begin to appear all over the surface. This will take anywhere from 2 to 3 minutes or more, depending on the consistency of the batter. Once bubbles appear on the surface, use the tip of a wide spatula to gently lift one side. Look at the bottom to see if it is evenly but lightly browned. If it is, slide the spatula under the entire pancake; turn it and cook the other side. When the pancakes are browned on both sides, remove one and test it by cutting into the center to see if it is done.

4. Keep them warm and sit down and eat.

It's perfectly acceptable to keep one batch (4 to 6 pancakes) warm in the oven while you cook a second batch. In that case, the pancakes will not be in the oven for more than 10 minutes—not enough time for them to get soggy. Once everyone has at least two or three pancakes, I sit down and eat my serving, before returning to the stove to cook another batch. This has the added advantage of allowing you to enjoy yourself, which makes the rest of the people at the table feel more comfortable too.

To keep pancakes warm, preheat the oven to 200° to 250°F. As the pancakes are cooked, transfer them to a baking sheet; cover lightly with foil and keep warm in the oven for about 10 minutes.

Additional Guidelines

Making the Batter

1. If a recipe calls for flour, make sure to spoon it lightly into a dry measuring cup—one made of plastic or metal (not glass) that allows you to level off the top with a knife. Do not dip the cup into the flour; that packs the flour down too much and may make the batter thicker than you want it to be.

2. Combine all the dry ingredients (flour, baking powder, baking soda, spices) in one large bowl. In a smaller bowl, stir together the liquid ingredients (eggs, milk or other liquid, melted butter) until blended. Then add the liquid ingredients to the dry all at once. If, for some reason, the batter seems too thick, add water or milk, 1 tablespoon at a time, gently stirring, until the consistency is right. I prefer a batter that is just a little thicker than heavy cream.

3. Stir—*never beat*—the ingredients together. Use a whisk, wooden spoon or rubber spatula and stir just until blended

and evenly moistened. Overmixing will develop the gluten in the flour and toughen the pancakes.

Essential Equipment

Griddle or skillet: A griddle pan is better than a skillet for cooking pancakes because its low edges make it easier to turn them and because you can cook quite a few at once. Many stoves come with a large rectangular griddle built into the top. These are usually heavy and of excellent quality.

Stovetop griddle pans have long handles and tough nonstick surfaces. They are reasonably priced, in the same range as a skillet. Many are large enough to fit over two burners. Buy one that is heavy enough to conduct the heat properly. If the griddle is too thin, it will heat unevenly or too quickly and cause the pancakes to burn.

Before I invested in a stovetop griddle pan, I used a large (12-inch) heavy nonstick skillet with low, slightly sloping sides. This design is far superior to a skillet with straight sides because it allows you to reach in and turn the pancakes.

An electric skillet or griddle (also nonstick) is convenient because you can double your output by heating up the electric skillet on the counter and the griddle or skillet on the stove, so two pancake chefs can work simultaneously.

Although I prefer to cook pancakes on a nonstick surface, it is not essential. A well-seasoned iron skillet conducts heat evenly and also turns out perfect pancakes.

Brush: A wide natural-fiber (not plastic) brush is handy for brushing the griddle or skillet with fat. The natural bristles will not melt when they come into contact with the hot surface, as plastic might. Natural-bristle brushes are also of better quality than the plastic ones and can be washed in the dishwasher or in hot soapy water over and over again.

A paper towel can also be used to rub a thin drizzle of oil over the surface of the pan.

Ladle: To ensure pancakes of uniform size, use a small ladle or a dry measuring cup (my preference) with a long (3-inch) handle. For each pancake, slowly pour the batter in one spot on the preheated surface. A ¼-cup ladle (or dry measuring cup) will make pancakes about 3 inches in diameter. Bigger pancakes can be made with a larger ladle or measuring cup.

Spatula: A thin, wide metal spatula or pancake turner works best. Plastic ones are suggested for a nonstick surface because they save the surface from scratches. Be sure their edges aren't too blunt: Thin or beveled edges make it easier to get under the pancake and turn it.

Freezing Pancakes

Although I wouldn't serve frozen pancakes on Sunday morning (after all, half the fun is making them!), kids love them for a snack after school or for a quick weekday breakfast. If you have pancakes left over, by all means freeze them. Separate them with pieces of foil and place them in a self-closing plastic bag. To reheat, place them on a baking sheet in a preheated oven or in a toaster oven (no need to thaw them) at 350°F for about 10 minutes.

Apple Cottage Cheese Pancakes

COTTAGE CHEESE makes these apple pancakes especially tender and fluffy. Served with warm applesauce and sprinkled with cinnamon sugar, they make an appealing breakfast. Cook the pancakes very slowly until they are lightly browned but cooked through.

1 cup low-fat cottage cheese

3 large eggs, *separated*

3 tablespoons unsalted butter, melted

½ teaspoon vanilla extract

1 cup peeled, cored and chopped apple

¼ cup plus 2 tablespoons unbleached
   all-purpose flour

2 tablespoons sugar

¼ teaspoon salt

   Cinnamon Sugar *(recipe follows)*

3 cups store-bought or homemade
   applesauce, warmed

1. In a large bowl, combine the cottage cheese, egg yolks, butter and vanilla. Stir to blend. Add the apple, flour, sugar and salt and stir to combine. In a separate bowl, beat the egg whites until soft peaks form. Gently fold into the batter just until blended.

2. Heat a large nonstick griddle or skillet over medium heat until hot enough to sizzle a drop of water. Brush with a thin film of vegetable oil, or spray with nonstick cooking spray. For each pancake, pour a scant ¼ cup batter onto the griddle or into the skillet. Adjust the heat to medium-low. Cook until the tops are covered with small bubbles and the bottoms are lightly browned. Carefully turn and lightly brown the other side. Repeat with the remaining batter.

3. Sprinkle the warm pancakes with Cinnamon Sugar and serve with warm applesauce.

MAKES ABOUT 16 3-INCH PANCAKES

Cinnamon Sugar: Combine ½ cup sugar and 1 teaspoon ground cinnamon in a small bowl. Stir to blend. Serve from a shaker.

Ban Pan O La with Café Navarro Mango Syrup

MASHED BANANAS MAKE THESE PANCAKES SING with banana flavor. The whole wheat flour lends a nice nutty taste, and the beaten egg whites folded into the batter lighten everything up. This recipe is from my son-in-law, Peter Dilcher, a manager at the cozy and colorful Café Navarro in Eugene, Oregon. Served with a warm mango sauce, the pancakes are a popular item from the café's weekend brunch menu.

1   cup unbleached all-purpose flour
1   cup whole wheat flour
1   tablespoon packed light brown sugar
1   teaspoon baking powder
½   teaspoon baking soda
½   teaspoon salt
2   large bananas, peeled and cut
    into chunks

1½   cups buttermilk *(or see page 25)*
½   cup vegetable oil
3   large eggs, *separated*
1   teaspoon vanilla extract

Café Navarro Mango Syrup *(recipe follows)*
    or sliced bananas or strawberries
    and warm maple syrup

1. Into a large bowl, sift together the flours, brown sugar, baking powder, baking soda and salt.

2. In the bowl of a food processor, puree the bananas, or mash them smoothly in a large bowl with a potato masher. Add the buttermilk, oil, egg yolks and vanilla. Process or whisk to blend.

3. Pour the banana mixture over the dry ingredients and stir just until blended. In a separate bowl, beat the egg whites until soft peaks form; gently fold into the batter just until blended.

4. Heat a large nonstick griddle or skillet over medium heat until hot enough to sizzle a drop of water. Brush with a thin film of vegetable oil, or spray with nonstick cooking spray. For each pancake, pour ¼ to ⅓ cup batter onto the griddle or into the skillet. Adjust the heat to medium-low. Cook until the tops are covered with small bubbles and the bottoms are lightly browned. Gently turn and cook until lightly browned on the other side. Repeat with the remaining batter.

5. Serve with Café Navarro Mango Syrup or with sliced fruit and warm maple syrup.

MAKES ABOUT 18 4-INCH PANCAKES

Café Navarro Mango Syrup: Puree 1 cup diced mango. If the mango is stringy, press it through a strainer. In a small saucepan, combine the mango, ⅓ cup water and 2 tablespoons sugar and heat, stirring, until heated through. Add 1 tablespoon fresh lime juice. Serve warm.

Banana Sour Cream Pancakes with Cinnamon Maple Syrup

A DAPTED FROM A RECIPE FROM BETTE'S OCEANVIEW DINER in Berkeley, California, these are melt-in-your-mouth moist and tender. The Cinnamon Maple Syrup is easy to assemble while the pancakes are slowly cooking.

4	large eggs	1-2	bananas, peeled and cut into thin slices
2	cups sour cream		
⅔	cup unbleached all-purpose flour		
2	teaspoons baking powder		Cinnamon Maple Syrup
½	teaspoon ground cinnamon		*(recipe follows)*
¼	teaspoon salt		

1. In a large bowl, whisk the eggs until light and bubbly. Stir in the sour cream until blended. Sift the flour, baking powder, cinnamon and salt onto the liquid ingredients. Fold until blended.

2. Heat a large nonstick griddle or skillet over medium heat until hot enough to sizzle a drop of water. Brush with a thin film of vegetable oil, or spray with nonstick cooking spray. For each pancake, pour a scant ¼ cup batter onto the griddle or into the skillet. Immediately arrange 3 or 4 thin slices of banana on the surface of each pancake. Adjust the heat to medium-low. Cook the pancakes slowly until the tops are covered with small bubbles and the bottoms are lightly browned. Carefully turn and cook until lightly browned on the other side. Repeat with the remaining batter.

3. Serve immediately with Cinnamon Maple Syrup.

MAKES ABOUT 12 4-INCH PANCAKES

Cinnamon Maple Syrup: Combine 1 cup maple syrup, 1 tablespoon unsalted butter and ½ teaspoon ground cinnamon in a small saucepan and cook, stirring to blend, until the mixture boils. Remove from the heat and let stand until ready to serve.

Blueberry Buttermilk Pancakes with Blueberry Sauce

T HESE ARE THE ULTIMATE blueberry buttermilk pancakes, studded with fresh berries and topped with blueberry sauce. The buttermilk makes them light and pleasantly tangy. Frozen berries can be substituted for the fresh. In place of the sauce, you can simply add fresh or frozen berries to warm maple syrup or honey.

2 cups unbleached all-purpose flour

1 tablespoon sugar

1 teaspoon baking soda

1 teaspoon salt

2 cups buttermilk
 (or see the following page)

3 large eggs, *separated*

4 tablespoons (½ stick) unsalted butter, melted

1½ cups blueberries, rinsed and sorted

Blueberry Sauce *(recipe follows)*, warm maple syrup or honey

1. Sift the flour, sugar, baking soda and salt into a large bowl. In a separate bowl, beat the buttermilk, egg yolks and butter until blended. In another bowl, beat the egg whites until soft peaks form.

2. Stir the buttermilk mixture into the flour mixture just until blended; there will still be some lumps. Add the blueberries. Add the egg whites and carefully fold just until blended.

3. Heat a large nonstick griddle or skillet over medium heat until hot enough to sizzle a drop of water. Brush with a thin film of vegetable oil, or spray with nonstick cooking spray. For each pancake, pour a scant ¼ cup batter onto the griddle or into the skillet. Adjust the heat to medium-low. Cook until the tops are covered with small bubbles and the edges appear to be setting. Turn and cook until golden brown on the other side. Repeat with the remaining batter.

4. Serve with Blueberry Sauce, warm maple syrup or warm honey.

MAKES ABOUT 16 4-INCH PANCAKES

Blueberry Sauce: Stir ⅓ cup sugar and 1 tablespoon cornstarch together in a medium saucepan. Add 1 pint (about 2 cups) sorted, rinsed blueberries. Heat, stirring, until the berries soften and the mixture thickens, about 5 minutes. Serve warm or at room temperature.

If you don't have buttermilk on hand, add lemon juice or cider vinegar to a measuring cup and add milk. To make 2 cups buttermilk, use 2 tablespoons lemon juice or cider vinegar and 2 cups milk. For 1½ cups buttermilk, use 1 to 2 tablespoons lemon juice or vinegar and add 1½ cups milk.

Buckwheat Pancakes
with Apricot Jam & Sour Cream

THIS IS MY VERSION OF BLINI, the famous Russian pancakes made with buckwheat flour. Buckwheat has a strong, distinctive flavor, especially when it is ground into flour. It also has a mildly sandy consistency, which is why I prefer to mellow its texture by mixing it with white flour. I like my buckwheat pancakes drizzled with melted butter, spread with apricot preserves that have been melted down to a saucelike consistency and topped with sour cream. This recipe makes a big batch.

1½ cups milk

1 package active dry yeast

1 cup unbleached all-purpose flour

1 cup buckwheat flour

1 teaspoon sugar

½ teaspoon salt

3 large eggs, *separated*

8 tablespoons (1 stick) unsalted butter, melted

2 tablespoons clarified unsalted butter (page 14), *optional*

8 tablespoons (1 stick) unsalted butter, melted

Sugar

1 cup apricot jam, or more as needed, warmed

About 1 pint sour cream

1. Heat the milk in a small saucepan until lukewarm; remove from the heat. Sprinkle the yeast over the top and let stand until softened, 2 to 3 minutes.

2. Meanwhile, sift the flours, sugar and salt into a large bowl.

3. In a separate bowl, whisk the egg yolks until creamy; stir in the milk mixture and the melted butter. Add to the dry ingredients and stir just until blended. Cover with plastic wrap and place in a warm spot until doubled in bulk, about 1 hour.

4. When the batter has risen, beat the egg whites in a medium bowl until soft peaks form. Gently fold into the batter just until blended.

5. Heat a large nonstick griddle or skillet over medium heat until hot enough to sizzle a drop of water. Brush with a thin film of vegetable oil or clarified butter, if using. Add the batter by tablespoons for small pancakes or use a scant ¼ cup measure for larger pancakes. Adjust the heat to medium-low. Cook until the tops are covered with small bubbles and the bottoms are lightly browned. Carefully turn and lightly brown the other side.

6. Keep the pancakes warm on a platter covered with foil in an oven set at the lowest temperature while you cook the remaining batter. To serve, drizzle each serving with some of the melted butter and sprinkle with sugar. Top with warm apricot jam and a spoonful of sour cream.

MAKES ABOUT 48 3-INCH PANCAKES

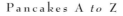

Corn Pancakes with Sour Cream & Caviar

T HESE SAVORY CORNMEAL cakes are moist, tender and speckled with fresh corn kernels. I love to eat them slathered with sour cream and topped with tiny spoonfuls of black caviar, which is exactly the way a similar corn cake is served at Arcadia restaurant in New York City. Serve as a first course or as a brunch dish. For a more traditional version, omit the onion and serve with sweet butter or warm maple syrup.

½ cup yellow cornmeal

½ cup unbleached all-purpose flour

¾ teaspoon baking soda

½ teaspoon salt

½ cup corn kernels, preferably fresh
(drained canned kernels may
be substituted)

1 tablespoon grated onion

Freshly ground black pepper

1 cup buttermilk *(or see page 25)*

2 large eggs, *separated*

4 tablespoons (½ stick) unsalted butter,
melted

1½ cups sour cream

2 ounces golden or black caviar

1. Into a large bowl, sift together the cornmeal, flour,
baking soda and salt. Add the corn, onion and a grinding
of black pepper; stir to coat.

2. In a small bowl, whisk the buttermilk, egg yolks and
2 tablespoons of the butter until blended. In a separate bowl,
beat the egg whites until soft peaks form.

3. Stir the buttermilk mixture into the dry ingredients just until blended.
Add the beaten whites and gently fold in just until blended.

4. Heat a large nonstick skillet or griddle over medium heat until hot enough to sizzle a
drop of water. Brush with a thin film of vegetable oil, or spray with nonstick cooking spray.
For each pancake, pour a scant ¼ cup batter onto the griddle or into the skillet. Adjust the
heat to medium-low. Cook until the tops are covered with small bubbles, the bottoms are
lightly browned and the edges are beginning to set. Carefully turn and lightly brown the
other side. Repeat with the remaining batter.

5. Brush the warm pancakes with the remaining 2 tablespoons melted butter. Top each
with 1 tablespoon sour cream and ½ teaspoon caviar and serve.

MAKES ABOUT 24 2-INCH PANCAKES

Cocoa Pancake-ettes with Susan's Fudge Sauce

ESPECIALLY FOR CHOCOHOLICS, these little silver dollars of tender chocolate topped with warm fudge sauce and a puff of unsweetened whipped cream are meant for dessert, not breakfast.

Make the excellent fudge sauce ahead; it'll keep, tightly covered and refrigerated, for up to one month. The sauce recipe is from my good friend Susan Westmoreland.

Susan's Fudge Sauce

- 1 cup unsweetened cocoa powder, preferably Dutch processed
- ¾ cup sugar
- ½ cup packed light brown sugar
- Pinch of salt
- ¾ cup heavy cream
- 8 tablespoons (1 stick) unsalted butter, cut into 8 pieces
- 1 teaspoon vanilla extract

Pancakes

- 1¼ cups unbleached all-purpose flour
- ¼ cup unsweetened cocoa powder, preferably Dutch processed
- 3 tablespoons sugar
- 1 teaspoon baking powder
- ¾ teaspoon baking soda
- ½ teaspoon salt
- 1 cup buttermilk *(or see page 25)*
- ¼ cup whole milk
- 1 large egg
- 2 tablespoons unsalted butter, melted
- ¼ cup mini chocolate chips

Confectioners' sugar
- 1 cup heavy cream, whipped

1. **To make Susan's Fudge Sauce:** Stir the cocoa, sugars and salt in a medium saucepan until blended. Stir in the cream; the mixture will be very thick. Add the butter. Cook, stirring constantly, until the mixture is smooth and comes to a boil. Remove from the heat and let stand for 5 minutes. Stir in the vanilla. Serve warm. The sauce will keep in the refrigerator for up to 1 month.

2. **To make the Pancakes:** Sift the flour, cocoa, sugar, baking powder, baking soda and salt into a large bowl. In a separate bowl, whisk the buttermilk, milk, egg and melted butter until blended. Add to the dry ingredients and gently fold until blended. Fold in the chocolate chips. Do not overmix.

3. Heat a large nonstick griddle or skillet over medium heat until hot enough to sizzle a drop of water. Brush with a thin film of vegetable oil, or spray with nonstick cooking spray. Add the batter by rounded tablespoons. Adjust the heat to medium-low and cook until bubbles begin to appear around the edges and the bottoms are lightly browned. If necessary, reduce the heat to low to prevent the pancakes from scorching or browning too fast. Carefully turn and lightly brown the other side. Repeat with the remaining batter. Reheat the fudge sauce, if necessary

4. Arrange the pancakes on dessert plates (about 4 per serving). Sprinkle lightly with confectioners' sugar. Drizzle with the warm fudge sauce. Spoon a little whipped cream onto the side of each plate. Serve warm.

MAKES 24 2-INCH PANCAKES

Cottage Cheese, Lemon & Strawberry Pancakes

WITH SLIVERS OF STRAWBERRY AND A TOUCH OF LEMON ZEST, these cottage cheese pancakes are as light in flavor as they are in texture. Serve with Lemon Sauce, warm honey or maple syrup. Garnish with sliced fresh strawberries.

2	large eggs, *separated*		Pinch of salt
⅔	cup cottage cheese	1	cup thinly sliced strawberries
¼	cup plus 2 tablespoons unbleached all-purpose flour		
2	tablespoons milk		Confectioners' sugar
2	tablespoons unsalted butter, melted		Lemon Sauce *(recipe follows)*, warm honey or maple syrup
2	tablespoons sugar	2	cups thinly sliced strawberries *(optional)*
1	teaspoon vanilla extract		
1	teaspoon grated lemon zest		

1. In a medium bowl, stir the egg yolks, cottage cheese, flour, milk, butter, sugar, vanilla extract, lemon zest and salt until blended.

2. In a separate bowl, beat the egg whites until soft peaks form. Carefully fold the whites into the batter just until blended. Add the 1 cup sliced strawberries and gently stir to combine.

3. Heat a large nonstick griddle or skillet until hot enough to sizzle a drop of water. Brush with a thin film of vegetable oil, or spray with nonstick cooking spray. For each pancake, pour a scant ¼ cup batter onto the griddle or into the skillet, making sure there are a few strawberry slices in each pancake. Adjust the heat to medium-low. Cook until the tops are covered with small bubbles and the bottoms are lightly browned, about 2 minutes. Carefully turn and lightly brown the other side of the pancake. Repeat with the remaining batter.

4. Sprinkle with confectioners' sugar or serve with Lemon Sauce, warm honey or maple syrup. Serve with additional sliced strawberries, if desired.

MAKES ABOUT 14 3-INCH PANCAKES

Lemon Sauce: In a small saucepan, combine ⅓ cup sugar and 2 tablespoons cornstarch until blended. Gradually stir in 1 cup water and the grated zest of 1 lemon. Heat, stirring, until the mixture thickens and boils. Add the strained juice of 1 lemon and 1 lemon, thinly sliced. Serve warm.

Dutch Baby with
Cardamom Honey Apples

S OMETIMES CALLED A POPOVER PANCAKE, this audacious-looking flapjack is made
in a large skillet. It puffs up, rising dramatically as it bakes in the oven. It is topped
with sautéed apple slices laced with ground cardamom and sweetened with honey. Golden
Delicious apples are best for this recipe because they keep their shape when cooked.

The pancake takes 18 minutes to bake—just enough time to put together the apple topping. (For a savory variation, see New Year's Eve Popover Pancake with Smoked Salmon & Dill Butter on page 62.)

Dutch Baby

3 large eggs
¾ cup milk
¾ cup unbleached all-purpose flour
1 tablespoon sugar
2 tablespoons unsalted butter

Cardamom Honey Apples

2 large apples (Golden Delicious)
1 tablespoon unsalted butter
½ teaspoon ground cardamom
½ cup honey
1 tablespoon fresh lemon juice

1. **To make the Dutch Baby:** Preheat the oven to 400°F. Place an 8-to-10-inch cast-iron skillet or other heavy skillet with a heatproof handle in the oven. 2. Combine the eggs, milk, flour and sugar in a medium bowl and whisk until smooth. Using a pot holder, remove the skillet from the oven and add the butter; tilt the pan to melt the butter and coat the skillet. Add the batter all at once and immediately return the skillet to the oven.

3. Bake until the pancake puffs up around the edges, 18 to 20 minutes.

4. **Meanwhile, make the Cardamom Honey Apples:** Peel, quarter and core the apples. Cut into thin wedges. Heat the butter in a medium skillet until sizzling. Add the apple wedges and cook, stirring gently, until lightly browned on both sides. Sprinkle with the cardamom and stir to coat. Add the honey and heat to boiling. Remove from the heat; stir in the lemon juice.

5. To serve the pancake, slide it from the skillet onto a large platter. Pour the Cardamom Honey Apples into the center. Cut into wedges and serve, distributing the filling evenly.

MAKES 4 SERVINGS

Egg Pancake

I SERVE THE ITALIAN VERSION of this simply made egg pancake as a light lunch, piled with baby salad greens that have been tossed with fresh lemon juice and olive oil, curls of Parmesan cheese and toasted walnuts. When I'm in the mood for Asian flavors, I make the same pancake with sesame oil, garlic, scallions and toasted sesame seeds. It, too, is delicious topped with salad greens. Or you can cut either version into ½-inch-wide strips and use it as a topping for stir-fried vegetables, stir-fried rice, rice salad or plain chicken broth. I sometimes make more than one and fold the pancakes into quarters and serve them for a snack, main dish or side dish.

2   large eggs

1   tablespoon cold water

2   teaspoons extra-virgin olive oil

1   small garlic clove, crushed
     through a press *(optional)*
     Pinch of salt

Freshly ground black pepper

5-6   leaves fresh Italian (flat-leaf) parsley,
       or about 1 teaspoon fresh oregano,
       thyme or rosemary leaves

1   tablespoon grated Parmigiano-
     Reggiano cheese

1. In a medium bowl, whisk the eggs, water, oil, garlic (if using), salt and pepper until well blended; let stand a few minutes until the foam subsides.

2. Heat a 10-inch nonstick skillet over medium heat until hot enough to sizzle a drop of egg. Brush with a thin film of vegetable oil, or spray with nonstick cooking spray. Add the batter to the pan all at once, tilting the pan and swirling the batter so it covers the bottom of the pan evenly.

3. After about 1 minute, sprinkle the parsley or other herbs over the pancake, pressing lightly into the soft surface. Cook, undisturbed, until the pancake is set, 3 to 4 minutes more. Sprinkle with the cheese, cover and cook for 1 minute more. Uncover and slide out of the pan onto a plate. Fold into quarters and serve, or roll up and cut into strips.

MAKES 1 LARGE PANCAKE OR 1 SERVING

Asian Egg Pancake: Make as above, except substitute dark sesame oil for the olive oil and 1 tablespoon very finely sliced green scallion tops and ½ teaspoon sesame seeds (optional) for the parsley. Omit the cheese and the last 1 minute of covered cooking. Serve as described in the headnote.

F

Fresh Corn Cakes with Tomato Salsa

THESE DELICATE, SAVORY CAKES, made with sour cream and fresh corn, are studded with bits of jalapeño pepper. They make a perfect summertime appetizer when ripe tomatoes and fresh corn are in season. In a pinch, they can be served with a good store-bought tomato salsa or black bean salsa. Or you can keep everything simple, forget the salsa and enjoy them plain.

¼ cup unbleached all-purpose flour

3 tablespoons yellow cornmeal

1 teaspoon baking powder

½ teaspoon salt

1 cup corn kernels, preferably fresh
   (or substitute canned kernels)

1 tablespoon minced fresh jalapeño
   pepper, or to taste

1 cup sour cream

3 large eggs

Tomato Salsa *(recipe follows)*
Cilantro leaves or other fresh
   herbs *(optional)*

1. In a large bowl, stir together the flour, cornmeal, baking powder and salt until blended. Add the corn and jalapeño and toss to coat.

2. In a separate bowl, whisk the sour cream and eggs until blended. Add to the dry ingredients and stir just until blended.

3. Heat a large nonstick griddle or skillet over medium heat until hot enough to sizzle a drop of water. Brush with a thin film of vegetable oil, or spray with nonstick cooking spray. For each pancake, pour a scant ¼ cup batter onto the griddle or into the skillet. Adjust the heat to medium-low. Cook until the tops are covered with small bubbles, the bottoms are lightly browned and the edges are set, about 4 minutes. Turn and cook until lightly browned on the other side, about 2 minutes more. Repeat with the remaining batter.

4. Serve warm with a spoonful of salsa on top of each. Garnish with herbs, if using.

MAKES ABOUT 14 3-INCH PANCAKES

Tomato Salsa: In a medium bowl, combine 2 cups diced ripe tomatoes, ¼ cup minced sweet onion, 2 tablespoons chopped fresh cilantro or basil, 1 tablespoon *each* extra-virgin olive oil and fresh lime or lemon juice, and salt and freshly ground pepper to taste. Let stand at room temperature until ready to serve.

Flannel Cakes with Raspberry Maple Syrup

S OFT, FLUFFY AND COMFORTING, these delicious pancakes are made by beating eggs and sugar with an electric mixer until they are light. The unusual technique contributes to the texture—hence their name. This old-fashioned recipe comes from Chicago chef Jolene Worthington.

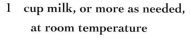

3 large eggs, at room temperature	1 cup milk, or more as needed, at room temperature
3 tablespoons sugar	3 tablespoons unsalted butter, melted
1½ cups unbleached all-purpose flour	
1½ teaspoons baking powder	
¾ teaspoon salt	**Raspberry Maple Syrup** *(recipe follows)*

1. In a large mixing bowl, beat the eggs and sugar on high speed until light and fluffy, about 5 minutes.

2. Sift the flour, baking powder and salt into a separate large bowl.

3. Gently stir the 1 cup milk and the butter into the egg mixture just until blended. Then pour the liquid ingredients over the dry. Gently fold the ingredients together until the dry ingredients are evenly moistened. If the batter seems thick, add more milk, 1 tablespoon at a time, to thin slightly. Do not overmix.

4. Heat a large nonstick griddle or skillet over medium heat until hot enough to sizzle a drop of water. Brush with a thin film of vegetable oil, or spray with nonstick cooking spray. For each pancake, pour ⅓ cup batter onto the griddle or into the skillet and spread evenly with the bottom of the cup. Adjust the heat to medium-low. Cook until the tops are covered with small bubbles and the bottoms are golden. Gently turn and cook until the pancakes are puffed and lightly browned. Keep the pancakes warm in an oven set at the lowest temperature while you cook the remaining batter.

5. Serve with Raspberry Maple Syrup.

MAKES ABOUT 12 5-INCH PANCAKES

Raspberry Maple Syrup: Combine 1 cup maple syrup and ½ cup unsweetened frozen (or fresh) raspberries in a small saucepan. Heat until the mixture begins to boil. Cool slightly. Press through a sieve to puree the berries into the syrup. Serve warm.

Ginger, Carrot & Sesame Pancakes

G RATED CARROTS, sesame seeds and ground ginger give these small pancakes their distinctively Asian taste. They are the perfect finger food with drinks before dinner or served as a side dish with grilled soy-marinated seafood or chicken. Once the ingredients are prepared, the pancakes go together and fry up very quickly. For the full flavor treatment, make sure to serve them with the Thai dipping sauce.

2 tablespoons sesame seeds

2 cups shredded carrots
(about 3 medium)

½ cup finely chopped scallions

2 tablespoons grated fresh ginger

1 garlic clove, crushed through a press

¼ cup cracker meal

2 large eggs, lightly beaten

1 teaspoon salt
Vegetable oil

Thai Dipping Sauce (page 93)

1. Toast the sesame seeds in a dry skillet over low heat, stirring, until golden, about 2 minutes.

2. Combine the carrots, scallions, ginger and garlic in a large bowl; stir to blend. Add the cracker meal, eggs, sesame seeds and salt; stir to blend.

3. Heat ½ inch oil in a medium skillet until hot enough to sizzle a crust of bread. Add the batter by rounded tablespoons and fry, turning once, until browned on both sides. Repeat with the remaining batter.

4. Serve warm with Thai Dipping Sauce.

MAKES ABOUT 20 BITE-SIZE PANCAKES

H

Heavenly Cloud Cakes

SOUR CREAM, eggs and flour make pancakes as light as air — so light that at Bette's Diner in Berkeley, California, these ethereal offerings are called Cloud Cakes. Serve with warm Berry Sauce or Raspberry Maple Syrup.

4   large eggs
2   cups sour cream
⅔   cup unbleached all-purpose flour
2   teaspoons baking powder
¼   teaspoon salt

Berry Sauce *(recipe follows)* or
    Raspberry Maple Syrup (page 41),
    warmed

1. In a large bowl, beat the eggs until they are thick and light in color. Gradually stir in the sour cream until blended. Sift the flour, baking powder and salt together into a separate bowl. Gradually stir the dry ingredients into the egg mixture.

2. Heat a large nonstick griddle or skillet over medium heat until hot enough to sizzle a drop of water. Brush with a thin film of vegetable oil, or spray with nonstick cooking spray. For each pancake, pour a scant ¼ cup batter onto the griddle or into the skillet. Adjust the heat to medium-low. Cook until the tops are covered with small bubbles and the bottoms are lightly browned. Carefully turn and cook until the other side is golden brown. Repeat with the remaining batter.

3. Serve with Berry Sauce or Raspberry Maple Syrup.

MAKES ABOUT 18
3-TO-4-INCH PANCAKES

Berry Sauce: Combine ¼ cup water and 1 tablespoon cornstarch in a small saucepan and stir until the cornstarch is dissolved. Add one 10-ounce box thawed frozen strawberries or raspberries in sweetened syrup. Heat, stirring, until the mixture boils and thickens. Remove from the heat and stir in 2 tablespoons orange liqueur, if desired.

Indian Spiced Red Lentil Cakes with Coconut Raita

THESE SPICY LITTLE CAKES are not truly Indian in origin, but they are so called because they use all the flavors that I love in Indian food: cumin seed, Madras curry powder, fresh ginger, browned onion and hot green pepper. The cakes can be made ahead and served at room temperature or reheated in a low oven. I like them as a side dish as part of an all-vegetable menu or with roasted meats or grilled fish. They are also good as a snack with a tall glass of iced tea or a frosty beer. Be sure to serve the Coconut Raita with them: It provides a cooling counterpoint to the spices in the pancake.

Lentil Cakes

1 cup red lentils (available in health-food and specialty markets)
3 tablespoons vegetable oil
¼ cup chopped onion
1 garlic clove, finely chopped
½ teaspoon whole cumin seed
1 teaspoon Madras curry powder
1 tablespoon seeded, chopped jalapeño or other hot chili pepper
1 tablespoon peeled, chopped fresh ginger
¼ teaspoon salt
2 large eggs, lightly beaten

Coconut Raita

1 cup plain whole-milk (or low-fat) yogurt
¼ cup peeled, finely chopped seedless cucumber
2 tablespoons unsweetened flaked coconut (available in health-food and specialty markets)

¼ cup coarsely chopped fresh cilantro, or more to taste

1. **To make the Lentil Cakes:** Combine the lentils and 6 cups water in a small saucepan; heat to boiling. Remove from the heat; cover and let stand for 1 hour. Drain well.

2. In a small skillet, heat the oil. Add the onion and cook, stirring, until lightly browned, about 3 minutes. Add the garlic and cumin and cook for 1 minute more. Add the curry powder and cook for 30 seconds more. Remove from the heat and cool slightly.

3. Meanwhile, combine the lentils, chili pepper, ginger and salt in a food processor and process to a coarse puree. Transfer to a bowl and stir in the sautéed onion mixture. Add the eggs and stir to blend.

4. Heat a large nonstick griddle or skillet over medium heat until hot enough to sizzle a drop of water. Brush with a thin film of vegetable oil, or spray with nonstick cooking spray. Add the batter by tablespoons and cook until the cakes are set, the tops are covered with small bubbles and the bottoms are browned. Carefully turn and brown the other side. Arrange on a large plate or tray. Repeat with the remaining batter.

5. **To make the Coconut Raita:** Combine the yogurt, cucumber and coconut. Place a spoonful on top of each pancake and garnish with a pinch of chopped cilantro. Serve warm.

MAKES ABOUT 24 3-INCH PANCAKES

John's Crepes with Mushrooms, Spinach & Cheese

THIS IS ONE OF MY STANDBY DISHES for week-end entertaining. The crepes can be made ahead, filled and refrigerated until just before you are ready to bake them.

12 crepes (page 51)

3 tablespoons extra-virgin olive oil

1-1¼ pounds mushrooms (a combination of white button, shiitake, oyster, portobello, chanterelles and/or whatever kind is available), rinsed, trimmed and thinly sliced (about 8 cups)

¼ cup finely chopped fresh Italian (flat-leaf) parsley

1 tablespoon fresh thyme leaves

1 garlic clove, finely chopped

Salt and freshly ground black pepper

1 10-ounce package fresh spinach, washed, stemmed and coarsely chopped

1 5-ounce package mild goat cheese, crumbled

2 cups shredded mozzarella cheese (8 ounces)

1. Make the crepes and set aside.

2. Preheat the oven to 350°F.

3. Heat the oil in a large skillet until hot enough to sizzle a slice of mushroom. Add the mushrooms all at once and cook, stirring, over medium-high heat until they begin to brown, about 10 minutes. Stir in the parsley, thyme, garlic, salt and pepper to taste. Cook for 1 minute.

4. Reduce the heat to medium and stir in the spinach. Cover and cook until just wilted, about 2 minutes. Uncover, add the goat cheese and stir until melted.

5. Spoon the mushroom mixture down the center of each crepe. Roll up the crepes and arrange them side by side in a 13-x-9-inch baking dish. Sprinkle with the mozzarella cheese. Cover the pan with foil and heat until the cheese melts, about 15 minutes. Serve warm.

MAKES 12 CREPES OR 4 SERVINGS

John's Basic Crepes

I FELL IN LOVE WITH CREPES and the person who would become my husband at about the same time. John's specialty was crepes spread with jam, rolled up and dusted with confectioners' sugar. He cooked and I ate. I was so impressed with his culinary skills and his attentions that it was some time before I realized that crepes are actually easy to make and take only a little patience to master.

The perfect crepe is so soft and delicate that it seems to melt in the mouth. They are also lovely filled with savory foods, such as mushrooms, spinach and goat cheese (page 49) and served as an entrée. Or they can be filled with ice cream or mousse or sweetened ricotta.

This recipe is for a basic crepe. The brandy lends a fragrant dimension, so add it if you have some on hand. Make the batter ahead of time and let it stand for at least an hour. Or, make it up one day ahead and refrigerate until ready to use. Crepes also freeze well. They are great to have on hand for entertaining or for last-minute suppers.

½ cup unbleached all-purpose flour	1 cup milk
½ teaspoon salt	2 tablespoons unsalted butter, melted
3 large eggs	1 tablespoon brandy *(optional)*

1. Combine the flour and salt in a medium bowl. In a separate bowl, whisk the eggs, milk, butter and brandy, if using, until blended. Add to the flour all at once and gently stir with the whisk until blended. Let stand for at least 1 hour at room temperature. (The batter can be refrigerated, covered, overnight; stir to blend before using.)

2. Heat a small (6-to-7-inch), heavy nonstick skillet or crepe pan over medium heat until hot enough to sizzle a drop of water. Brush with a thin film of vegetable oil, or spray with nonstick cooking spray. Ladle about 3 tablespoons batter (or a scant ¼ cup measure) into the hot pan and quickly tilt to coat the pan and make a thin pancake.

3. Cook the crepe until the edges begin to curl and the underside is golden, about 1½ minutes. Loosen the edges of the crepe with a thin flexible spatula or a heatproof rubber spatula and gently turn. Cook the underside until lightly spotted with color, about 30 seconds. Turn the crepe out onto a wire rack.

4. Repeat with the remaining batter, stirring it occasionally. As the crepes are made, transfer them from the rack to a pie plate. Cover lightly with a piece of foil and keep warm in an oven set at the lowest temperature. The crepes can be cooled, wrapped in foil and refrigerated for a few days before reheating in a warm oven. They can also be frozen for at least 1 month. Cool, stack them on top of one another and wrap tightly in foil and then in a freezer bag. (The crepes need no paper between them; they will not stick together when frozen or refrigerated.) They thaw at room temperature in about 1 hour and can be reheated right in the foil (in a 350°F oven for 15 minutes) without unwrapping.

MAKES 15 6-INCH CREPES

Ricotta-Filled Crepes with Berry Sauce: Mix together a 15-ounce container of ricotta cheese, ½ cup confectioners' sugar, 1 teaspoon vanilla extract, ½ teaspoon grated orange zest, a pinch of ground nutmeg or cinnamon and ¼ cup minced candied orange rind or citron (optional). Fill 12 crepes with the mixture. Drizzle with Berry Sauce (page 45).

K

Kaiserschmarren with Plum Compote

(Emperor's Scrambled Pancake)

KAISER'S SCHMARREN translates as "the Emperor's scrambled pancake." A more apt description might be "egg and raisin pancake with plum compote." The recipe was given to me by my good friends Ulrike Tatzl and Kit Traub, who describe it fondly as a beloved Viennese specialty. Ulli found the recipe in an old book of handwritten recipes from her Austrian family. I enjoy it for lunch, but Ulli says it can also be dessert. The technique may seem a little odd at first, for it is not a typical preparation. Because the pancake is so thick and tender, it has to be broken into pieces to be turned, creating more surfaces for browning. The browned sugar and eggs give this wonderful pancake its soft and crunchy texture and caramelized-sugar taste.

¾ cup milk	2 tablespoons unsalted butter
3 large eggs, *separated*	½ cup dark raisins
½ cup unbleached all-purpose flour	
Pinch of salt	Confectioners' sugar
2 tablespoons sugar	Plum Compote *(recipe follows)*

1. Whisk the milk and egg yolks in a large bowl until blended. Stir in the flour and salt until blended. Do not overmix. In a separate bowl, beat the egg whites until foamy. Gradually beat in the sugar until soft peaks form. Carefully fold the beaten whites into the batter just until blended.

2. Heat the butter in a 10-inch nonstick skillet until the foam subsides. Add the batter all at once. Sprinkle with the raisins. Cover and cook, without stirring, over low heat until the bottom is lightly browned and set (the top will be still be soft), about 3 minutes.

3. Uncover. Using 2 wide spatulas, turn the pancake over in sections. It will break into pieces, but that is all right. The object is to lightly brown the puffed top section. As it browns, pull the pancake apart into 1-to-2-inch sections with 2 forks, and then push it back together in the skillet. Cover and cook 1 minute more.

4. Invert a plate over the skillet and, protecting your hands with mitts, flip the pancake out of the skillet onto the plate. Sprinkle with confectioners' sugar and serve warm with Plum Compote.

MAKES 2 SERVINGS

Plum Compote

(*Zwetschkenroester*)

1 pound purple (Italian) plums, rinsed,
  stemmed, halved and pitted

¼ cup sugar

1 cinnamon stick

2 whole cloves

Place the plums in a medium saucepan and add just enough water to cover. Stir in the sugar and add the cinnamon and cloves. Bring to a boil, stirring to dissolve the sugar. Reduce the heat and simmer the plums until tender, but not falling apart, about 10 minutes. Cool to room temperature. Transfer to a bowl and remove the whole spices. Serve with the *Kaiserschmarren*.

Luscious Lemon Pancakes

N O COLLECTION OF PANCAKE RECIPES would be complete without this one, and no other lemon pancake could be quite as delicious. The recipe is adapted from Marion Cunningham's *The Breakfast Book* (Alfred A. Knopf, 1987).

3   large eggs, *separated*

¼   cup unbleached all-purpose flour

¾   cup low-fat cottage cheese

4   tablespoons (½ stick) unsalted
     butter, melted

2   tablespoons sugar

¼   teaspoon salt

1   tablespoon grated lemon zest

Confectioners' sugar and
     mixed fruit (sliced strawberries,
     blueberries and raspberries) or
     warm maple syrup

1. In a large bowl, combine the egg yolks, flour, cottage cheese, butter, sugar, salt and lemon zest. In a separate bowl, beat the egg whites until soft peaks form. Carefully fold the beaten whites into the batter just until blended.

2. Heat a large nonstick griddle or skillet over medium heat until hot enough to sizzle a drop of water. Brush with a thin film of vegetable oil, or spray with nonstick cooking spray. For each pancake, pour a scant ¼ cup batter onto the griddle or into the skillet. Adjust the heat to medium-low. Cook until the tops are covered with small bubbles and the bottoms are lightly browned. Carefully turn and lightly brown the other side. These cook quickly. Repeat with the remaining batter.

3. Serve sprinkled with confectioners' sugar, accompanied by sliced fruit, or with warm maple syrup.

MAKES ABOUT
12 3-INCH PANCAKES

Latkes

(Potato Pancakes)

HANUKKAH WOULDN'T BE THE SAME without this recipe from Betty Chernetz, mother of my friend and colleague Barbara Chernetz. The secret to perfectly crisp potato pancakes is frying in melted vegetable shortening. I serve them as a meal at nonholiday times by accompanying them with a generous portion of unsweetened applesauce and a spoonful of sour cream.

3 large all-purpose potatoes (about 1¾ pounds), peeled	Freshly ground black pepper
1 small onion	About ½ cup solid vegetable shortening (such as Crisco)
1 large egg, lightly beaten	
2 tablespoons matzo meal	Applesauce
1 teaspoon salt	Sour cream

1. Grate the potatoes with a medium-fine grater into a large bowl. Grate the onion and add to the potatoes. Carefully drain any liquid in the bowl. (This is important!)

2. Add the egg, matzo meal, salt and pepper to the potato mixture; stir to blend.

3. Heat ½ cup of the shortening in a heavy skillet over high heat until it ripples. For each pancake, spoon 1 rounded tablespoon batter into the oil. Fry until crisp and browned; turn and brown the other side. Adjust the heat if necessary if the pancakes are browning too fast. Repeat with the remaining batter, adding more shortening, if needed.

4. Serve immediately with applesauce and sour cream.

MAKES ABOUT 24 BITE-SIZE PANCAKES

Little Crunchy Rice Pancakes

T O GET A NICE CRUNCH on the outside, cook these in a shallow pool of hot oil. You can add 2 tablespoons snipped sun-dried tomatoes or ½ cup sautéed chopped mushrooms to the rice mixture.

1 tablespoon olive oil, or more as needed	2 large eggs, beaten
¼ cup chopped onion	½ cup shredded mozzarella cheese
1 garlic clove, crushed through a press	¼ cup grated Parmigiano-Reggiano cheese
2 cups soft cooked rice (from ⅔ cup raw)	2 tablespoons snipped fresh parsley
	Freshly ground black pepper

1. Combine the 1 tablespoon oil and the onion in a skillet and cook, stirring, over low heat until the onion is golden, about 3 minutes. In a small bowl, combine the onion mixture, garlic and rice.

2. Add the eggs, mozzarella, Parmigiano-Reggiano, parsley and a generous grinding of black pepper. Stir to blend.

3. Heat a large nonstick griddle or skillet over medium heat until hot enough to sizzle a drop of water. Add a thin layer of olive oil. Add the rice mixture by heaping tablespoons. Cook the pancakes until brown and crispy; turn and brown the other side, adding a drizzle more of oil to the pan, if needed. Repeat with the remaining batter.

4. Serve warm.

MAKES ABOUT 12 3-INCH PANCAKES

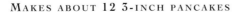

Mashed Potato Pancakes

DON'T PASS THESE BY, assuming that they're just leftover mashed potatoes shaped into cakes. I have jazzed them up with shredded cheese, mustard and scallion and added beaten eggs to lighten them a little. Serve as a side dish, instead of plain boiled or roasted potatoes, with grilled or broiled meats or poultry.

1 pound russet potatoes, unpeeled	1 teaspoon prepared mustard
1 cup shredded Emmentaler, Gruyère or other Swiss cheese (4 ounces)	½ teaspoon salt Freshly ground black pepper
2 large eggs, beaten	1 tablespoon vegetable oil or butter,
1 scallion, trimmed and thinly sliced	or more as needed

1. Cook the potatoes in boiling, salted water until tender, about 20 minutes; drain and cool slightly. When cool enough to handle, slip off the skins and roughly mash in a large bowl.

2. Add the cheese, eggs, scallion, mustard, salt and pepper to taste to the potatoes. Stir to blend with a wooden spoon. With wet hands, form the potatoes into patties about 3 inches wide and ½ inch thick. Rinse your hands frequently to prevent sticking.

3. Heat a large nonstick griddle or skillet over medium heat until hot enough to sizzle a drop of water. Add the 1 tablespoon oil or butter. When hot, add the patties and cook until browned and crisp on the bottoms. Then turn and brown the other side. Repeat with the remaining patties, adding more oil as needed.

4. Serve warm.

MAKES ABOUT 12 3-INCH PANCAKES

New Year's Eve Popover Pancake with Smoked Salmon & Dill Butter

FOR YEARS, we entertained friends after midnight at a New Year's breakfast. This easy-to-make pancake was often on the menu. The batter is a simple combination of eggs, milk and flour that is baked in a preheated skillet. As the pancake cooks, it puffs up, the inside remaining soft and the outside cooking to a crunchy crust. Served with plenty of "bubbly," with smoked salmon and fresh dill on top, the pancake is sensational, and utterly simple to make.

Popover Pancake

3 large eggs
¾ cup milk
¾ cup unbleached all-purpose flour
1 tablespoon snipped fresh dill
½ teaspoon salt
  Grinding of black pepper
2 tablespoons unsalted butter

Topping

2 tablespoons unsalted butter, melted
3-4 slices smoked salmon
¼ cup fresh dill sprigs
2 tablespoons minced sweet onion
  (optional)

1. **To make the Popover Pancake:** Preheat the oven to 400°F. Place an 8-to-10-inch cast-iron skillet or other heavy skillet with a heatproof handle in the oven.

2. Combine the eggs, milk, flour, dill, salt and pepper in a bowl and whisk until smooth. Using a pot holder, remove the skillet from the oven and add the butter; swirl the pan to melt the butter and coat the skillet. Add the batter all at once and immediately return the skillet to the oven.

3. Bake until the pancake puffs up around the edges, 18 to 20 minutes.

4. **To top the Pancake:** Cut the pancake into wedges and drizzle with a little melted butter. Top each with a slice of smoked salmon and a few dill sprigs. Add a little minced onion, if using, and serve.

MAKES 3 OR 4 SERVINGS

Onion & Cumin Crepe

A LARGE SWEET ONION slowly cooked in olive oil until golden and caramelized gives this crepe a nutty dimension. Ground cumin, a familiar flavor in both Mexican and Indian cooking, adds a spicy touch. I like to make a couple of these at a time and serve them in wedges as part of an all-vegetable menu. The pancake is also good cut into squares and eaten as a snack.

2 tablespoons extra-virgin olive oil	Salt and freshly ground black pepper
1 large (about 1 pound) sweet onion, halved lengthwise, thinly sliced and separated into half-rings (about 2½ cups)	3 large eggs
	¼ cup milk
	¼ cup unbleached all-purpose flour
1 teaspoon ground cumin	
1 garlic clove, crushed through a press	Mixed green salad *(optional)*

1. Heat the oil over medium-low heat in a medium (10-inch) nonstick skillet. Add the onion and cook, stirring, until browned, about 12 minutes. Stir in the cumin, garlic, salt and pepper to taste; cook, stirring, for 1 minute. Spread the mixture out in an even layer; remove from the heat.

2. Whisk the eggs and milk in a small bowl until blended. Add the flour and ½ teaspoon salt and whisk just to blend; set aside.

3. Place the skillet over medium heat. When the onions are sizzling, add the batter and tilt the pan to cover the onions evenly. Adjust the heat to medium-low and cook until the crepe is set and nicely browned on the bottom, 4 to 5 minutes. Using 2 spatulas, carefully turn the crepe. Or, if preferred, place a large plate over the skillet and, using a large towel to protect your hands, invert the skillet onto the plate and then slide the pancake back into the hot skillet. Cook the other side for 1 to 2 minutes to brown.

4. Turn the crepe out onto a plate. To serve, cut into wedges, and serve topped with salad, if desired.

MAKES 1
8- OR 9-INCH CREPE
OR 2 6-INCH CREPES
2 TO 4 SERVINGS

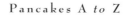

Pecan Pancakes with
Buttered Pecans & Warm Maple Syrup

THE FLAVORS OF PECANS AND MAPLE have a natural affinity for each other. Sprinkle the warm butter-coated pecans over the pancakes and drizzle with the warm maple syrup. Vanilla ice cream, sliced bananas and buttered pecans also make a fabulous filling for dessert crepes (see John's Basic Crepes, page 51), topped with warm maple syrup.

½ cup chopped pecans

1 tablespoon sugar

1½ cups unbleached all-purpose flour

2 teaspoons baking powder

½ teaspoon salt

1¼ cups milk

2 large eggs, *separated*

2 tablespoons unsalted butter, melted

1 teaspoon vanilla extract

Buttered Pecans

4 tablespoons (½ stick) unsalted butter

1 cup coarsely chopped pecans

1 cup warmed maple syrup, or more as needed

Whipped cream *(optional)*

1. Combine the pecans and sugar in a food processor and finely chop. Sift the flour, baking powder and salt into a large bowl. Stir in the pecan mixture.

2. In a medium bowl, whisk together the milk, egg yolks, butter and vanilla. Add to the flour mixture and stir just until blended. Beat the egg whites in a medium bowl until soft peaks form. Gently fold into the batter just until blended.

3. Heat a large nonstick griddle or skillet over medium heat until hot enough to sizzle a drop of water. Brush with a thin film of vegetable oil, or spray with nonstick cooking spray. For each pancake, pour a scant ¼ cup batter onto the griddle or into the skillet. Adjust the heat to medium-low. Cook until the tops are covered with small bubbles and the bottoms are lightly browned. Carefully turn and cook until lightly browned on the other side. Repeat with the remaining batter.

4. **Meanwhile, make the Buttered Pecans:** Melt the butter in a medium skillet. Add the pecans and cook, stirring, until lightly browned, about 3 minutes. Spoon the warm pecans over the pancakes and serve with warmed maple syrup and dollops of whipped cream, if desired.

MAKES ABOUT 15 5-INCH PANCAKES

Quinoa & Company Pancakes

Quinoa, bulgur and toasted almonds keep each other company in these crunchy, half-dollar-size savory cakes. They are perfect as a side dish with meat, poultry or seafood. The recipe was inspired by one from chef Danny Smith of John Andrew's Restaurant in South Egremont, Massachusetts.

½ cup quinoa, rinsed and drained	½ cup milk
½ cup bulgur	2 large eggs, *separated*
½ cup natural (unblanched) almonds	¼ cup unbleached all-purpose flour
1 tablespoon unsalted butter	1 teaspoon salt
½ cup finely chopped onion	
1 garlic clove, crushed through a press	

1. Heat a medium (10-inch) nonstick skillet with a tight-fitting lid over medium-high heat. Add the quinoa and cook, stirring, until it is no longer moist and begins to brown, about 3 minutes. Add 1 cup water and bring to a boil. Reduce the heat to medium-low, cover and cook until the water is absorbed, about 15 minutes. Uncover and cool.

2. Meanwhile, combine the bulgur and 1 cup boiling water and let stand, covered, until the bulgur is softened, about 20 minutes. Drain well.

3. Finely chop the almonds and toast them in a dry skillet over low heat, stirring, until golden, about 5 minutes. Cool.

4. Combine the quinoa, bulgur and almonds in a large bowl. Melt the butter in a small skillet and cook the onion until golden, about 5 minutes. Add the garlic and cook for 1 minute more. Add to the quinoa mixture.

5. In a small bowl, whisk the milk and egg yolks together until blended. Stir into the quinoa mixture. Add the flour and salt and stir to blend.

6. In a separate bowl, beat the egg whites until soft peaks form. Gently fold into the batter just until blended.

7. Heat a large nonstick griddle or skillet over medium heat until hot enough to sizzle a drop of water. Brush with a thin film of vegetable oil, or spray with nonstick cooking spray. Drop the batter by rounded tablespoons onto the griddle or into the skillet. Using the back of the spoon, spread the batter into 2½-inch rounds. Cook until the tops are covered with small bubbles and the bottoms are lightly browned, about 2 minutes. Turn and lightly brown the other side. Keep warm in an oven set at the lowest temperature while you cook the remaining cakes.

MAKES ABOUT 24 3-INCH PANCAKES

Rux's Family's Favorite Pancakes

CALLED "BATTER CAKES" by the family of my editor, Rux Martin, this old-fashioned recipe calls for cubes of fresh, firm-type sliced bread, which keep the pancakes very tender. Serve with any of your favorite toppings. Rux's family likes melted fresh fruit jam or a fresh berry syrup.

6 slices Pepperidge Farm white bread, crusts trimmed, cut into ½-inch cubes	2 large eggs
	4 tablespoons (½ stick) salted butter, melted
¼ cup unbleached all-purpose flour	
1 tablespoon sugar	1 cup strawberry, raspberry,
1½ teaspoons baking powder	mixed berry or other favorite jam,
¾ cup milk	or more as needed *(optional)*

1. In a large bowl, combine the bread, flour, sugar and baking powder.

2. In a separate bowl, whisk the milk and eggs together until blended. Stir in the melted butter. Add the liquid ingredients to the dry ingredients. Stir to blend. Let stand for 5 min-

utes so the bread can absorb some of the liquid. Stir thoroughly, breaking up some of the bread cubes.

3. Heat a large nonstick griddle or skillet over medium heat until hot enough to sizzle a drop of water. Brush with a thin film of vegetable oil, or spray with nonstick cooking spray. For each pancake, pour a scant ¼ cup batter onto the griddle or into the skillet. Adjust the heat to medium-low. Cook until the bottoms are lightly browned, then carefully turn and lightly brown the other side. Repeat with the remaining batter.

4. Heat the jam, if using, in a small saucepan until it melts. Drizzle over the pancakes and serve.

MAKES ABOUT 14 3-INCH PANCAKES

Rich Raspberry Sour Cream Pancakes

S OUR CREAM AND RASPBERRIES are both luxury foods: the first rich, the second expen-
sive. But for special occasions, both ingredients are worth every calorie and every cent.
Make these during the late summer when plump, ripe, locally grown berries are in the farm-
ers' markets. Then top with fresh sugared berries and confectioners' sugar or Raspberry
Maple Syrup.

1 cup unbleached all-purpose flour	½ pint (about 1 cup) raspberries, rinsed and well drained
½ teaspoon baking soda	
½ teaspoon salt	
1 large egg, lightly beaten	Confectioners' sugar
1¼ cups sour cream	½ pint (about 1 cup) raspberries, rinsed and well drained, and, if desired, mixed with 1 tablespoon sugar or to taste, *optional*
3 tablespoons milk	
½ pint (about 1 cup) raspberries, rinsed and well drained (dry on a kitchen towel or doubled paper towel)	Raspberry Maple Syrup (page 41), *optional*

1. Sift the flour, baking soda and salt into a large bowl. In a separate bowl, whisk the egg,
sour cream and milk until blended.

2. Add the liquid ingredients to the dry ingredients and carefully fold together; the batter will be thick.

3. Heat a large nonstick griddle or skillet over medium heat until hot enough to sizzle a drop of water. Brush with a thin film of vegetable oil, or spray with nonstick cooking spray. For each pancake, pour a scant ¼ cup batter onto the griddle or into the skillet. Adjust the heat to medium-low. As bubbles appear on the surface, top each pancake with 4 or 5 berries, pressing them down into the batter. Carefully turn and cook the other side until lightly browned. Repeat with the remaining batter.

4. Garnish with the remaining ½ pint raspberries, if using, and sprinkle with confectioners' sugar, or serve with Raspberry Maple Syrup.

MAKES ABOUT 12 4-INCH PANCAKES

Sam's Superb Swedish Pancakes

A T THE FORT, a restaurant in Denver, Colorado, chef-owner Sam Arnold serves these large, thin crepes rolled around a pile of wild Montana huckleberries and sprinkled with a snowy blanket of confectioners' sugar. Sam admits that frying the first crepe can be a little tricky. Use a large, flat, flexible spatula to reach in, then turn it with confidence.

I like to make big (about 9-inch) pancakes, fill them with sweetened berries and serve one for each person. This makes a very impressive brunch dish.

3   large eggs
1   cup milk, or more as needed
3   tablespoons unsalted butter, melted
     Pinch of salt
1½ cups unbleached all-purpose flour

Berry Filling
2   pints strawberries, rinsed

1   pint (about 2 cups) blueberries,
     rinsed and sorted
½   pint (about 1 cup) raspberries, rinsed
¼   cup sugar
2   tablespoons fresh lime juice

Confectioners' sugar
1-2 cups sour cream or crème fraîche

1. In a large bowl, whisk the eggs, the 1 cup milk, the butter and salt until blended.

2. With a whisk, gradually stir in the flour until the batter is smooth. Add small amounts of milk, as needed, to thin the batter to the consistency of heavy cream. Set aside.

3. **Make the Berry Filling:** Slice the strawberries into a large bowl. Add the blueberries and raspberries. Sprinkle with the sugar and lime juice. Set aside at room temperature.

4. Heat a large (8-to-10-inch) nonstick skillet or crepe pan over medium heat until hot enough to sizzle a drop of water. Brush with a thin film of vegetable oil, or spray with non-stick cooking spray. Pour ½ cup batter into the pan and immediately tilt the pan so that the batter coats the bottom to the edges. Adjust the heat to medium-low and cook until the pancake is set and the bottom begins to brown. Carefully turn the pancake and cook the other side, about 1 minute. Turn the pancake out of the pan onto a platter. Keep warm in an oven set at the lowest temperature while you cook the remaining batter.

5. To serve, spoon about ¾ cup Berry Filling down the center of each pancake and loosely roll it up. Place on a large platter or arrange on individual serving plates. Using a sieve or sugar shaker, sprinkle generously with confectioners' sugar. Use any extra fruit filling as a garnish. Pass a bowl of sour cream or crème fraîche.

MAKES 8 6-INCH PANCAKES OR 4 10-INCH PANCAKES

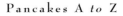

Sweet Corn Cakes

ADD A FEW BLUEBERRIES to these breakfast corn pancakes made with cornmeal and fresh corn kernels, or top with any fresh berries. *(See the photograph on the cover.)*

½   **cup yellow cornmeal**

½   **cup unbleached all-purpose flour**

2   **tablespoons sugar**

½   **teaspoon baking soda**

½   **teaspoon salt**

1   **cup corn kernels, preferably fresh (drained canned kernels may be substituted)**

1   **cup buttermilk** *(or see page 25)*

2   **large eggs**

2   **tablespoons unsalted butter, melted**

Warmed maple syrup or confectioners' sugar and sugared berries

1. Into a large bowl, sift together the cornmeal, flour, sugar, baking soda and salt. Add the corn; stir to coat.

2. In a small bowl, whisk the buttermilk, eggs and butter until blended.

3. Stir the buttermilk mixture into the dry ingredients until just blended. Do not overmix.

4. Heat a large nonstick griddle or skillet over medium heat until hot enough to sizzle a drop of water. Brush with a thin film of vegetable oil, or spray with nonstick cooking spray. For each pancake, pour a scant ¼ cup batter onto the griddle or into the skillet. Adjust the heat to medium-low. Cook until the tops are covered with small bubbles, the bottoms are lightly browned and the edges begin to set. Carefully turn and cook until the other side is lightly browned. Repeat with the remaining batter.

5. Serve with maple syrup, or sprinkle with confectioners' sugar and serve with berries.

MAKES ABOUT 16 3-INCH PANCAKES

T

T.O.M.'s Famous Sunday Morning Pancakes

OUR GOOD FRIEND JOHN COBURN, affectionately called T.O.M. (aka "the old man") by his sons, serves these pancakes as a Sunday morning ritual. Make them plain or add fresh or individually frozen unsweetened raspberries or blueberries. If John doesn't have the berries on hand, he uses chopped apple. Serve with copious quantities of warm maple syrup.

1 cup unbleached all-purpose flour	1 cup fruit (raspberries, blueberries,
½ teaspoon baking soda	sliced strawberries or chopped,
½ teaspoon salt	peeled apple)
1 cup sour cream	
1 cup milk	Warm maple syrup
1 large egg	

1. Sift the flour, baking soda and salt into a large bowl. In a separate bowl, whisk the sour cream, milk and egg until blended.

2. Add the liquid ingredients to the dry ingredients and carefully fold together.

3. Heat a large nonstick griddle or skillet over medium heat until hot enough to sizzle a drop of water. Brush with a thin film of vegetable oil, or spray with nonstick cooking spray. For each pancake, pour a scant ¼ cup batter onto the griddle or into the skillet. Adjust the heat to medium-low. As bubbles appear on the surface, sprinkle each pancake with about 1 tablespoon fruit. Cook until the edges are set and the bottoms are golden brown. Turn and lightly brown the other side. Repeat with the remaining batter.

4. Serve with warm maple syrup.

MAKES ABOUT 14 4-INCH PANCAKES

U

Upside-Down Pineapple Pancakes with Pineapple Coconut Syrup

THIS RECIPE from Chef Philippe Padovani is a breakfast specialty at the Manele Bay Hotel on Lanai, one of the Hawaiian Islands. The pancake is similar to pineapple upside-down cake: Rings of fresh pineapple are sautéed in butter and brown sugar, topped with batter and baked in a hot oven. Canned pineapple rings can be substituted for fresh.

Use two 6-inch nonstick skillets (crepe pans are good) so you can make two pancakes at once. Otherwise, make one and repeat the process.

1 cup unbleached all-purpose flour

1 teaspoon sugar

½ teaspoon baking soda

½ teaspoon salt

2 tablespoons unsweetened flaked
   coconut (available in health-food
   and specialty stores)

4 tablespoons (½ stick) unsalted butter

¾ cup buttermilk *(or see page 25)*

¼ cup whole milk

1 large egg

2 tablespoons packed light brown sugar

4 canned pineapple rings, halved
   (reserve the juice for Pineapple
   Coconut Syrup)

Pineapple Coconut Syrup
(recipe follows)

1. Sift the flour, sugar, baking soda and salt together into a large bowl; add the coconut. Melt 2 tablespoons of the butter. In a separate bowl, whisk the butter, buttermilk, milk and egg until blended. Add to the dry ingredients and stir just until blended. Do not overmix.

2. Preheat the oven to 450°F, with a rack on the bottom.

3. Have ready 2 6-inch nonstick skillets or crepe pans with heat-resistant handles. Place 1 tablespoon of the remaining butter in each skillet and melt over low heat. Sprinkle 1 tablespoon of the brown sugar into each skillet and heat, stirring, until bubbling.

4. Arrange 4 halved pineapple rings in the bottom of each skillet. Heat the pans until the butter is sizzling. Add the batter to the skillets, dividing it evenly.

5. Bake the pancakes in the oven until their tops are firm when pressed lightly with a fingertip, 5 to 6 minutes. Making sure to protect your hand with a mitt, invert the pancakes onto a plate. If you are making 1 pancake at a time, cover the cooked pancake with foil to keep warm while making the next one.

6. Serve with Pineapple Coconut Syrup.

MAKES 2 6½-INCH PANCAKES OR 2 GENEROUS SERVINGS

Pineapple Coconut Syrup

½ cup canned unsweetened pineapple juice (reserved from the canned pineapple rings)

1 tablespoon cornstarch

½ cup coconut milk, preferably unsweetened

½ cup milk

Combine the pineapple juice and cornstarch in a small saucepan and stir until blended. Add the coconut milk and milk. Heat, stirring gently, until the mixture thickens slightly. Remove from the heat. Serve warm or at room temperature.

V-Ingredient Pancakes

THE PANCAKE FOR THE 22ND LETTER of the alphabet borrows its name from the Roman numeral for the number five. With just five ingredients, these easy-to-make cakes are perfect slathered with soft butter and drizzled with a little warm syrup or heated fruit jam.

1	cup milk	
3	tablespoons salted butter	
1½	cups unbleached all-purpose flour	
2½	teaspoons baking powder	
2	large eggs	

Softened butter for topping
Warm maple syrup or warmed
   fruit jam or jelly

1. In a small saucepan, heat the milk and butter until the butter is melted; cool. Sift the flour and baking powder into a large bowl. In a smaller bowl, whisk the eggs until blended; add the cooled milk mixture. Stir the liquid ingredients into the dry ingredients just until blended. Do not overmix.

2. Heat a large nonstick griddle or skillet over medium heat until hot enough to sizzle a drop of water. Brush with a thin film of vegetable oil, or spray with nonstick cooking spray. For each pancake, pour a scant ¼ cup batter onto the griddle or into the skillet. Adjust the heat to medium-low. Cook until the tops are covered with small bubbles and the bottoms are lightly browned. Carefully turn and lightly brown the other side. Repeat with the remaining batter.

3. Slather with softened butter and drizzle with warm maple syrup or warmed fruit jam or jelly.

MAKES ABOUT **20 3**-INCH PANCAKES

Wheat Germ & Buttermilk Cakes
with Peach & Cinnamon Maple Topping

T HESE LIGHT AND FLUFFY pancakes get just the right amount of crunch from wheat germ. Peaches are delicious on top of these pancakes when in season, but apples can be used instead.

1½	cups unbleached all-purpose flour
½	cup wheat germ
2	tablespoons sugar
1	teaspoon salt
½	teaspoon ground cinnamon
½	teaspoon baking soda
1¾	cups buttermilk, or more as needed *(or see page 25)*
4	tablespoons (½ stick) unsalted butter, melted
1	large egg

Topping

1	tablespoon unsalted butter
2	large peaches, peeled and cut into thin wedges
1	tablespoon fresh lemon juice
½	teaspoon ground cinnamon
½	cup maple syrup, or more to taste

1. Combine the flour, wheat germ, sugar, salt and cinnamon in a large bowl. Sieve the baking soda into the flour mixture. Stir to blend.

2. In a separate bowl, whisk the 1¾ cups buttermilk with the butter and egg until blended. Add to the flour mixture and stir just until blended. If the batter thickens too much while standing, stir in a little more buttermilk, about 1 tablespoon at a time, to thin slightly.

3. Heat a large nonstick griddle or skillet over medium heat until hot enough to sizzle a drop of water. Brush with a thin film of vegetable oil, or spray with nonstick cooking spray. For each pancake, pour ¼ cup batter onto the griddle or into the skillet. Adjust the heat to medium-low. Cook until the tops are covered with small bubbles and the bottoms are lightly browned. Carefully turn and cook the other side until lightly browned. Repeat with the remaining batter.

4. **Meanwhile, make the Topping:** Melt the butter in a medium skillet over medium-low heat. Add the peaches and cook, stirring, to coat and heat through. Sprinkle with the lemon juice and cinnamon. Stir to coat. Add the maple syrup and stir to blend. Gently heat. Do not boil.

5. Serve the pancakes warm with the warm topping.

MAKES ABOUT 12 4-INCH
PANCAKES

Whole Wheat Apple-Raisin Pancakes with Apple Cider Syrup

APPLE, RAISINS and earthy whole wheat flour make a nice trio of flavors in these pancakes. For a real taste of autumn, serve with fresh Apple Cider Syrup.

1½ cups unbleached all-purpose flour
½ cup whole wheat flour
2 tablespoons sugar
1 teaspoon baking soda
1 teaspoon ground cinnamon
1 teaspoon salt
2 cups peeled, cored and diced apples

¾ cup dark raisins
2 cups buttermilk *(or see page 25)*
3 large eggs, *separated*
2 tablespoons unsalted butter, melted
1 teaspoon vanilla extract

Apple Cider Syrup *(recipe follows)*

1. Sift the flours, sugar, baking soda, cinnamon and salt into a large bowl. Add the apples and raisins; toss to coat. In a separate bowl, stir the buttermilk, egg yolks, butter and vanilla until blended. In another bowl, beat the egg whites until soft peaks form.

2. Stir the buttermilk mixture into the flour mixture until the dry ingredients are just moistened. Add the beaten egg whites and gently fold in just until blended.

3. Heat a large nonstick griddle or skillet over medium heat until hot enough to sizzle a drop of water. Brush with a thin film of vegetable oil, or spray with nonstick cooking spray. For each pancake, pour a scant ¼ cup batter onto the griddle or into the skillet. Adjust the heat to medium-low. Cook until the tops are covered with small bubbles and the bottoms are golden brown. Carefully turn and lightly brown the other side. Repeat with the remaining batter.

4. Serve the pancakes with Apple Cider Syrup.

MAKES ABOUT **24** 4-INCH PANCAKES

Apple Cider Syrup: Combine ½ cup sugar and 2 tablespoons cornstarch in a medium saucepan and stir until well blended. Gradually stir in 2 cups apple cider until blended. Add 1 cinnamon stick and heat, stirring occasionally, to boiling. Cover and cook over low heat for 10 minutes. Remove from the heat and grate a little nutmeg into the syrup. Remove the cinnamon stick before serving.

XS (Extra-Small) Pancakes

MY SISTER-IN-LAW, Brenda Morris, encouraged her children to eat breakfast by treating them to extra-small pancakes. One day, the family invited a young friend to stay overnight. The next morning, after the boy had gone home, his embarrassed mother called to apologize for his behavior. It seems he had bragged to her that he'd eaten 36 pancakes. She was relieved to learn they were only an inch in diameter!

You can use any basic batter for these button-size pancakes, but this three-grain batter is especially good.

½ cup unbleached all-purpose flour

½ cup whole wheat flour

⅓ cup old-fashioned or quick-cooking oatmeal

2 teaspoons baking powder

½ teaspoon salt

¾ cup milk

1 large egg

2 tablespoons packed dark brown sugar

1 teaspoon vanilla extract

Warm maple syrup or honey

Sliced fruit, such as strawberries, bananas and/or peaches and nectarines *(optional)*

1. Combine the flours, oatmeal, baking powder and salt in a large bowl. Stir to blend.

2. In a separate bowl, whisk the milk, egg, brown sugar and vanilla until blended. Add the liquid ingredients to the dry ingredients and stir just until blended.

3. Heat a large nonstick griddle or skillet over medium heat until hot enough to sizzle a drop of water. Brush with a thin film of vegetable oil, or spray with nonstick cooking spray. Drop the batter by scant tablespoons for tiny pancakes (use a ¼-cup measure for larger pancakes). Adjust the heat to medium-low. Cook until the tops are covered with small bubbles and the bottoms are lightly browned, about 2 minutes. Turn and lightly brown the other side.

4. Keep the pancakes warm on a pie plate in an oven set to the lowest temperature while you cook the remaining batter. Serve with warm maple syrup or warm honey and sliced fresh fruit, if desired.

MAKES ABOUT 36 TINY PANCAKES OR 16 3-INCH PANCAKES

Yogurt, Pear & Lemon Pancakes with Caramelized Pear Compote

T HESE MOIST, TENDER PANCAKES are dotted with chopped pears and topped with a luscious mixture of sliced pears sautéed in butter and sugar. They make a nice brunch.

Caramelized Pears

4	tablespoons (½ stick) unsalted butter
3-4	large ripe Bartlett pears, peeled, quartered, cored and cut into ½-inch wedges
2	tablespoons sugar
½	teaspoon ground cinnamon

Vanilla Yogurt Drizzle

1	cup plain low-fat yogurt
2	tablespoons sugar
1	teaspoon vanilla extract

Pear Pancakes

1½	cups unbleached all-purpose flour
2	tablespoons sugar
2	teaspoons baking powder
½	teaspoon baking soda
¾	cup plain low-fat yogurt
¾	cup milk
1	large egg
1	teaspoon grated lemon zest
1	cup peeled, cored and chopped pears

1. **To make the Caramelized Pears:** Heat the butter in a large nonstick skillet until it begins to foam. Add the pears and sprinkle with the sugar and cinnamon. Cook, gently turning, over medium heat until the sugar caramelizes and the pears are glazed, about 5 minutes. Set aside.

2. **To make the Vanilla Yogurt Drizzle:** Whisk the yogurt, sugar and vanilla in a small bowl until smooth. Let stand at room temperature until ready to serve. Or, if making ahead, return to room temperature before serving.

3. **To make the Pear Pancakes:** Sift the flour, sugar, baking powder and baking soda into a large bowl. In a separate bowl, whisk the yogurt, milk, egg and lemon zest until blended. Add to the dry ingredients and stir just until blended.

4. Heat a large nonstick griddle or skillet over medium heat until hot enough to sizzle a drop of water. Brush with a thin film of vegetable oil, or spray with nonstick cooking spray. For each pancake, pour a level ¼ cup batter onto the griddle or into the skillet. Reduce the heat to medium-low. Cook until the tops are covered with small bubbles and the bottoms are lightly browned. Sprinkle each pancake with about 1 tablespoon of the chopped pears; press in lightly. Carefully turn the pancakes and cook the other side until lightly browned. Repeat with the remaining batter.

5. Spoon Caramelized Pears on top of the pancakes. Pass Vanilla Yogurt Drizzle on the side.

MAKES ABOUT 12 4-INCH PANCAKES

Zucchini-Ginger Pancakes with Thai Dipping Sauce

I SERVE THESE IN THE SUMMER when I can buy fresh zucchini from farmstands. The shredded zucchini adds a little moisture, making these pancakes softer and less crunchy than the Ginger, Carrot & Sesame Pancakes on page 42. They are very good as a snack with drinks. Make them ahead and freeze, then reheat them in a moderate oven just until sizzling. For added zip, serve them with Thai Dipping Sauce on the side.

2 cups coarsely shredded zucchini (about 2 medium)
½ cup coarsely shredded carrots
½ cup finely chopped scallions
2 tablespoons grated fresh ginger
¼ cup cracker meal or matzo meal

2 large eggs, lightly beaten
½ teaspoon salt
Vegetable oil

Thai Dipping Sauce
(recipe follows)

1. Combine the zucchini, carrots, scallions and ginger in a large bowl; stir to blend. Add the cracker or matzo meal, eggs and salt; stir to blend.

2. Heat ¼ inch oil in a large skillet until hot enough to sizzle a crust of bread. Add the batter by rounded tablespoons and fry, turning, until lightly browned on both sides. Repeat with the remaining batter.

3. Serve warm with Thai Dipping Sauce. These are great made ahead and frozen. To reheat, spread the frozen pancakes on a nonstick baking sheet and place in preheated 300°F oven for 15 to 20 minutes.

MAKES ABOUT
24 2-INCH PANCAKES

Thai Dipping Sauce

Traditionally served with spring rolls, spiced meat dishes wrapped in lettuce leaves—and now with zucchini pancakes!

¼ **cup soy sauce**
¼ **cup fish sauce**
¼ **cup fresh lime juice**
2 **tablespoons sugar**

2 **tablespoons thinly sliced hot chili pepper (jalapeño or serrano are good)**
1 **garlic clove, minced**

Combine the soy sauce, fish sauce, lime juice, ¼ cup hot water, sugar, chili pepper and garlic in a small bowl. Serve at room temperature.

Index